650 | Tales of New York

Edited by Edward McCann

650 | WHERE WRITERS READ

Founder / Editor • Edward McCann
Executive Producer • Richard Kollath
Literary Ombudsman • Steven Lewis
Director of Operations • Jane Kaupp
Design Director • Diane Fokas
Social Media Strategist • Shayna Miller
Director of Photography • Kevin O'Connor
Chief Audio Engineer • Jesse Chason
Videography / Photography • Sara Caldwell
Copy Editor • Kathleen Stanley
Technical Advisor • Conrad Trautmann
Technical Advisor • Stephen Kaupp

Production Assistants

Robert Dennison, Lynn Dennison, Mackenzie Meeks,
Jackie Mercurio, Brian Reagher, and Isabella Fokas

Advisory Committee

Rachel Aydt, Laura Shaine Cunningham, Angela Davis-Gardner,
Karen Dukess, Joseph Goodrich, David Masello, Honor Molloy,
Irene O'Garden, John Pielmeier, Gretchen Reed, James Russek,
Angela Derecas Taylor and Julie Trelstad

"I look out the window and I see the lights and the skyline and the people on the street rushing around looking for action, love, and the world's greatest chocolate chip cookie, and my heart does a little dance." —*Nora Ephron*

ABOUT 650

There simply is no place in the world like New York. It's been described as "the biggest collection of villages in the world," and the old noir film *The Naked City* opened with this line: "There are eight million stories in this city... " We've selected just ten New York stories, representing each borough at least once, and hope you enjoy the ride.

650 is a celebration of writing and the spoken word, a literary forum for personal stories performed five minutes—and 650 words—at a time. Our events at theaters, colleges, and libraries around the country are organized around single, broad topics that invite a range of expression, and recorded performances are added to a digital archive of writers reading their work aloud. The writers and their work receive additional exposure through podcasts, broadcasts, our YouTube channel, and in these printed volumes.

650 features graduate students and grandparents, first-timers and bestsellers. It's all about the writing, with an emphasis on craft. It's about the choice of one word over another, about the shape of sentences and paragraphs, the arc of a narrative, the poetry of a unique literary voice. If you love language and enjoy a good story, you've come to the right place. To submit your work or attend our shows, visit our website or Facebook page, and join our mailing list.

Please tell your friends about 650, and spread the word about the spoken word.

Ed McCann

Edward McCann, Founder / Editor

READ650.COM
FACEBOOK.COM/READ650

CONTENTS

650 | Tales of New York

Edited by Edward McCann

DAVID MASELLO

David Masello moved to New York more than thirty years ago from Evanston, Illinois, and he has made his living as a writer and editor ever since. He began his career as a nonfiction book editor at Simon and Schuster, then went on to hold senior editorial positions at many magazines, including *Travel & Leisure, Art and Antiques,* and *Town and Country*, where he was features editor. He's currently executive editor of *Milieu*, a magazine about design and architecture. He's a widely published essayist and poet, with pieces appearing in the *New York Times, Salon, Best American Essays*, and numerous literary and art magazines. His plays have been produced and performed by the Manhattan Repertory Theatre, Jewish Women's Theatre of Los Angeles, Big Apple Theatre Festival, and Fresh Fruit Festival. He is the author of two books about art and architecture.

TAKING A NEW DIRECTION

David Masello

My first day after being fired from an unpleasant job began with a visit to the unemployment office, followed by a lunch invitation to New York's fanciest private club. Both events were firsts in my life.

I arrived at the club after a run across town, my suit pockets bulging with Labor Department literature—brochures on dressing for success and "Attitude and Job Performance."

Before we sat for lunch, the hostess, a newish friend, took me and two of her other friends to the club's library. Fifth Avenue traffic was a whispering whoosh behind floor-to-ceiling windows. A couple on a settee made a voice-cracking toast, "To France!" When a waiter asked for our drinks order, Katie, a financial manager, replied, "Tomato. Ice. Lemon. Please."—not an unreasonable or haughty directive, but said with an assurance I found admirable and unsettling.

Soon after we entered the club's ladies dining room, I the only man, in walked Brooke Astor, the then 99-year-old philanthropist and society figure. Even there, where diners' ancestors have streets

1

and parks named for them, the room quieted and energized with her entrance. People asked their tablemates for cues when it was okay to turn and verify the sighting, take in the contours of her hat.

My friend knew Mrs. Astor and took us to her table. I shook Mrs. Astor's white-gloved hand, through which, akin to braille, I felt a network of veins.

My friend told Mrs. Astor I was starting a literary magazine.

"Marvelous," Mrs. Astor said in a gritted high-Park Avenuese. "We do need another journal of letters."

Such plans were only marginally true. I did want to publish a journal called First Person, filled with personal essays, but I hadn't gotten past Xeroxing submissions from friends. I held my suit jacket close to my body as I leaned over to shake her hand goodbye, fearful that the addendum about "Pregnancy and Benefits Eligibility" might fall on her paprikaed sole.

As one of my lunch companions prepared to return to her job as a Times reporter, Katie to resume managing the assets of a family for whom streets and parks were named, and my hostess to work on a screenplay about her CIA directive father, I foresaw an afternoon in my fifth-floor walkup hunting down all twelve Combat roachtraps I had secreted years earlier. Although I had been removed from office life for only a day, I felt that everyone in the club suspected I was heading home for an episode of "Judge Judy."

As we left the club, Katie and I walked the same direction, but I sensed she was eager to break free. How odd I probably seemed to her. She must meet many men my age, partners in established firms, handsome, chronometer-watched alphas who dine in their own clubs and hire people to find roachtraps in their second homes. At an intersection, she asked, "Which way," curling her thumb like a hitchhiker to indicate uptown, downtown. I figured whichever direction I chose, she'd say the opposite.

"Downtown."

"Oh, I'm headed uptown," she said smoothly.

She offered me her cashmered paw. She shook with a smart once up, once down motion, reslung her cape and took off, the sidewalk reverberating with her heel-heavy departure.

I retraced the blocks we had walked. Near Fifth, I saw Brooke Astor leaving the club, struggling to keep open the door against a strong gust. I held it for her. With one hand, she secured her hat, its wide brim a current of rip-tide ripples.

"Thank you," she said, "A frightful wind." She was unable to look me in the eye because the gusts were so furious, ankle-stinging whirlpools of trash spinning on the sidewalk. I was just a kindly stranger. Her driver folded her into the backseat and when the door was closed, the small part I had played in her day had ended.

The corner I had been standing on was one of those that's perpetually windy—a result of the positioning of buildings, Central Park, circumstances unknown. But the moment I turned onto Fifth, it was again calm, a tranquil spring day. I no longer had to close my eyes to the wind. Suddenly, for the first time in my years in Manhattan, with no office to return to, I realized I could go in any direction I wanted.

MARTIN KLEINMAN

Martin Kleinman is New York City story teller. He has told his tales of real New Yorkers in his short fiction collection, *Home Front,* (Sock Monkey Press 2013) and on his blog *The Real New Yorkers,* as well as in the *Huffington Post,* and in venues all around New York City. A native New Yorker, he has lived in four of the five boroughs. After twenty five years in Park Slope, he moved to the northwest Bronx. Marty recently completed a second book on workplace innovation trends, is finishing a second collection of short fiction, and remains an international marketing communications consultant.

BOROUGH OF CHURCHES

Martin Kleinman

My wife and I moved to Brooklyn in 1985 and, two years later, our beautiful son was born. We lived in a bright, sunlit corner apartment, three-quarters up the slope of Park Slope. From our living room window, we were surrounded by three church steeples clustered at the corner of St. John's Place and Seventh Avenue.

I'll never forget the look on my grandma's face when I told her we were headed to Brooklyn. "Why?" she asked, trembling, as if I said I was moving to the fires of hell. For her part, she fled the fires of persecution in Russia and came to New York in 1913. Sixty years later, my parents had to drag Granny from her home in the south Bronx, kicking and screaming all the way. Once again, she had to flee. This time, it was the fires of arson, and the murders, a matter of life or death.

I moved from the Bronx as well. White flight wreaked havoc on my working class enclave in University Heights. Back then, most people decamped for Jersey or Westchester. No one moved to Brooklyn. People from The Bronx didn't even socialize with

Brooklynites.

But I was "city" through and through. Years later, after stints in Manhattan and Jackson Heights —when it was time to "settle down"—I found a new home. It was a Brooklyn neighborhood where newcomers cherished city life as much as I did.

I was amazed by Brooklyn. It was rough and tough, but the people had heart. And the view! From our windows, from our pitched tar rooftop, we saw, we smelled, we heard our harbor. New York was a seaport! You'd never know it, living up in the Bronx. Gulls, ferries, barges, ocean liners—there they were! There was the Statue of Liberty—so close!

There was no denying it, though. Of all the sights in my new Brooklyn, the view of the World Trade Center was the centerpiece.

The Towers were so majestic. I'd look out my living room window and see them, just beyond the churches, standing fast against the winds off the river, preening in the sun.

On 9/11, I lost a neighbor. He worked at Cantor. That chaotic blue sky morning, soon after the Towers were struck, his wife and I passed each other on the street. I was rushing back from school with my son. She was rushing to the school to pick her two kids up. We looked in each other's eyes as we passed. We spoke not a word. We just knew. Her husband, and thousands more, were gone.

In the ensuing days, a yellow cast hung over my Brooklyn neighborhood. The air was foul with the smell of a massive electrical fire, but worse. It was the stench of a crematorium.

I was derailed, lost. One day, maybe it was the Thursday

after the attacks, I sat on a park bench after walking my dog, deep in thought, so angry, confused and desperate for answers. A fellow dog owner from the park stopped and asked if I was okay.

I just put my face in my hands, too embarrassed to cry. My neighbor sat down with me. Silently, she put her hand upon my shoulders and I released a torrent of sobs. Finally, we talked a bit and laughed about some silly dog-related thing.

Brooklyn was called the "borough of churches." I understand what that really means. A place of worship is made of stone and glass. But it is much more. It is people, it is a community, with neighbors who understand and, when needed, reach out and help. It's about faith, and hope and heart.

My son was born here. After he left at eighteen, to start the great adventure of his life, he came right back. He has seen it all, from incredible poverty to equally incredible wealth. He is comfortable no matter what the social context or circumstance. He's a good balanced kid with a head on his shoulders and a wise-cracking Brooklyn mouth.

Someday, he may choose to leave, but it won't be because he has to flee.

MARIE PROELLER HUESTON

Marie Proeller Hueston is a freelance writer whose work has appeared in *O, Town & Country, Art & Auction, and Country Living.* She is the author of six decorating books including *Country Living Cottage Style* and *House Beautiful Decorating With Books* as well as two children's books: *The All-American Jump and Jive Jig* and *Christmas Eve with Mrs. Claus.* She blogs about home-improvement topics for *BobVila.com* and about the fun and frustrating moments of parenting for *NickMom.com.* Marie received a B.F.A. in photography and printmaking from Cornell University and an M.A. in American Folk Art Studies from NYU. Born and raised on Staten Island, Marie now lives on the other side of the Narrows, in Carroll Gardens, Brooklyn, with her husband, son, and daughter.

THE OUTSIDERS

Marie Proeller Hueston

Growing up in a German family in the middle of an Italian-American neighborhood on Staten Island meant always being a bit of an outsider. In a circle around my childhood home were the following families: The Argentos, the Palladinos, the Ingalineras, the Verdiglionis, the Santos, the DeSantos, the Muratoris, the Parlangelis, and the Vasciminis. We were the Proellers. Our father spoke with an accent, but not an Italian accent. He smoked a pipe.

This was the 1970s, the era of big American cars like the Lincoln Continental and the Ford LTD. Most of our neighbors had at least two of these cars parked in the driveway, one for each parent. And if a twenty-something son or daughter lived at home, there might also be a Trans Am or a Camaro. We had one family car—a powder-blue Volkswagen station wagon. It had two doors, a hatchback, and windows in the back seat that didn't roll down. Riding in my friends' cars felt like being in a living room on wheels.

Our house was furnished with Danish Modern and lithographs of 19th-century German scenes hung on the walls. In the kitchen you were more likely to find a pot of pea soup simmering on the stove (complete with a pig's knuckle) than spaghetti and meatballs. My mother shopped at Karl Ehmer, a German specialty store on New Dorp Lane, and made sandwiches for my brothers and me with aromatic salami or liverwurst spread on thick, buttered slices of rye bread. I used to beg her for Wonder Bread. She never gave in.

Christmas was the time of year when my family's differences were most prominently on display to the outside world. In the weeks following Thanksgiving, our neighbors' homes lit up one by one with colorful lights and large, illuminated plastic figurines: Frosty the Snowman, choirboys in red and white robes, or the entire Nativity scene. My favorite was Santa's sleigh being pulled by reindeer on the Vasciminis' roof. I'd stare out the window at this winter wonderland and wish we could string lights somewhere, too.

Our own holiday finery consisted of a single front-door wreath that we made ourselves with branches clipped from a giant yew bush in the yard. Inside there was an advent wreath—also homemade—on the dining-room table. Even though we bought our tree weeks before the 25th like everyone else, ours stood on the porch until Christmas Eve when we would bring it in to decorate. While I may have coveted much of my neighbors' extravagance, I do have to admit that, once trimmed, our tree was prettier than anyone's. (We're German—we invented the Christmas tree!)

After a childhood spent feeling different from those around me, my opportunity to blend in with the crowd finally presented itself when I got to high school—or so I thought. Venturing into Manhattan to attend Stuyvesant, I remember thinking that surely in the most diverse city in the world my classmates would not merely be German or Italian, but a veritable melting pot of New York City's ethnic communities.

I arrived at school on the first day, ready to be accepted by my fellow New Yorkers. "Hi, I'm Marie. I'm from Staten Island!"

It was at that moment that I realized what would become a lifelong truth: To most New Yorkers, Staten Island is as exotic a locale as Seattle or Saginaw. Being born and raised there means always being a bit of an outsider.

JOHN GREDLER

John Gredler, poet and memoirist, is a frequent contributor to 650 who's been writing in notebooks and journals for most of his adult life. He honed his craft at the Writing Institute at Sarah Lawrence College, Bella Villa Writers, 125, and the Terzo Piano Workshops. A recipient of the 2014 Gurfein Fellowship from The Writing Institute at Sarah Lawrence College, John's work has been published in *Atticus Review, Fictionique, Narratively, Dan's Papers, Westchester Review,* and *Talking Writing.* John lives and writes in Tuckahoe, New York.

SRO

John Gredler

I now had the second floor at 38 East Third to myself, a
mattress on the floor, my radio cassette player and piles of books
on either side. Not much else, not even a chair. Two tall windows
faced the brick wall of the neighboring building with the faded
letters spelling Provenzano Lanza Funeral Home painted on it.
A small garden below allowed morning light to come in and the
sounds of traffic to echo constantly day and night.

During the day I went to work at a single room occupancy
hotel down the block. Most of the tenants were drinkers, older, all
were white, the majority with Irish surnames, Callahan, Quigley,
Blackburn, Wedlock.

The first big job was to clear out the back yard. It had been
used as a dump for decades, piled high with furniture, shattered
cast iron bathtubs, rotting clothes, endless beer cans and empty
green pint bottles of Night Train and Wild Irish Rose.

Next was cleaning and painting the small grime encrusted

rooms of the SRO. Starting with the window, spraying the amber panes of glass, watching the dark yellow rivulets of nicotine tinted fluid mix with the blue Windex to form a greenish liquid that pooled on the sill, spilling over the edge and down the wall to the floor.

I was working there only three weeks when Old Carl died. He had been bedridden the entire time. Carl had a long beard and looked emaciated, but the few times I saw him alive he always nodded hello. He had cancer but did not want to go to the hospital. Mister Morgan and Ed Blackburn would help him out, getting him food and cigarettes or the bottle of Night Train he still managed to get down every day.

Then Morgan came to me and said Carl would not answer his door. I got his key and we opened it, the smell of heavy nicotine layered over the odor of Carl's unclean body, beneath that the sharp acidic smell of urine rising up from the floor.. I could see right away he was dead, his body stiff, his head turned up and away in an odd contortion, facing the wall. He appeared to be looking for something, or as if he was caught in a spasm of pain or of ecstasy before he died.

Morgan murmured "He's gone" then turned to shuffle away. The sunlight coming into the room was muted by the yellowed shade. I touched him on his wrist not to see if he had a pulse but out of a morbid curiosity. His arm was like a piece of dry wood, his long nailed fingers curled in like talons

Later a cop stood at the open doorway without going inside.

"He looks dead all right" he said before calling into the precinct on his radio. "I'll have to stay outside the room until the coroner gets here, could be a while."

I got a chair for the cop to sit on. It wasn't until after 9 P.M. that the black van marked NYC Coroner pulled up in front. Two men came in with a gurney, put Carl in a body bag and carried him out. The next day I went in to clear out his room. Under his bed were six mason jars full of urine, two without tops, in varying shades from dark amber to pale yellow.

A month later it was Morgan who would not answer his door. He had gone into the hospital for an infection in his foot and was told he might lose it if the antibiotics didn't work. "I'm not gonna be no peg leg". While he was recovering he stayed in bed. I would knock on his door to ask if he needed anything from outside.

His thin pale face with a bulbous nose wore a constant doubtful expression that made me think of a cartoon character, though I could never recall which. He always insisted on tipping me a dollar or two when I came back from the bodega. Like most of the tenants when they weren't drunk, Morgan was unfailingly courteous.

The morning he didn't answer I got the key and opened his door to see him propped up in bed with a plastic bag over his head, tied at the neck. I stood for a moment unable to move, not comprehending. I stepped in and saw he was not breathing. A large red upside down heart covered his face, the black lettering that I knew spelled 'I Love New York' crinkled and unreadable.

15

STEVEN LEWIS

Steven Lewis, Literary Ombudsman for Read650, is a columnist at *Talking Writing*, and a member of the Sarah Lawrence College Writing Institute faculty. A longtime freelancer, his work has been published in *The New York Times, The Washington Post, Christian Science Monitor, the Los Angeles Times, Ploughshares, Spirituality & Health* and others. Recent novels include *Take This, Loving Violet,* and *A Hard Rain,* all from Codhill Press, and Finishing Line Press published Steve's poetry chapbook, *If I Die Before You Wake.* His backlist includes *Zen and the Art of Fatherhood, The ABCs of Real Family Values, The Complete Guide for the Anxious Groom,* and *Fear and Loathing of Boca Raton (a Hippie's Guide to the New Sixties).* He divides his time between his writing space in New Paltz, New York and Hatteras Island, North Carolina.

STREET TAWK

Steven Lewis

As my late Aunt Miriam might have said, my old boyhood pal—let's call him Richard—has one filty mout. And what's more is that she would have known precisely what to do about his unseemly and unexpurgated vocabulary: Aunt Miriam was a no-nonsense grade school teacher from Queens ... she'd grab a bar of Ivory to suds out every four-letter word on his salty tongue.

No matter that Richard is sixty-eight, a father, a grandfather.

That said, if my tough-as-nails Aunt Miriam and my rough talking hipster friend Richard went chin to chin (which, by the way, would require a step stool for my pint-sized aunt), my money would be on my foul talking pal. Miriam would barely get the wrapper off the bar of soap before he'd blow her off the step stool with a barrage of obscenities—use your imagination—that she had never before heard, even from my Uncle Mac. It would be an f-ing massacre.

Richard is many things New York street—street photographer,

silkscreen artist of the streetwise, former owner of a hand lettering/ silk screen business on West 24th St., limo driver on the potholed avenues, parking lot attendant on N. Moore, tough talker. These days he reps for a guy in a heavily tattooed automobile world in the burbs he calls The Land of Tonys. Over the nearly five and a half decades that I've known him, the man has cursed out anyone and everyone who has crossed him on his path: hallway, lobby, elevator, sidewalk, subway ... from the bottom of the line (a railroad flat on 14th St.) all the way to the top of the line (The Dorilton on 71st and Broadway) as well as in that sometimes gratuitous world in between (living "rent-deferred" in a loft on Maiden Lane in lower Manhattan).

Up here in the momandapplepie Hudson Valley, where one rarely hears a discouraging or filthy word, I occasionally distract myself from the playful deer and antelope with a vision of my old pal racing back and forth on the Gowanus in his '63 white Porsche 356B, a mouth full of expletives-not-deleted aimed at anyone who deigns to cut him off. Or tailgate him. Or flip him the bird. And be assured that no one who cuts him off—or tailgates—or flips that bird—gets away unsullied by the effluvial deluge of my friend's profanities.

So it was surprising—damn surprising, actually—to hear him say recently that at the f-ing end of another f-ing day spent bs-ing with some a-hole Tonys, my old pal finally met his match. Not with a particular Tony, mind you. They don't get over on him. Not with his ex-wife. Nor with his girlfriend.

Just hours into a love-hate relationship with his brand new iPhone, Richard pushed a button and a woman's voice asked sweetly:

"What can I help you with?" Richard, being Richard, brought the device close to his mouth and grumbled some obscene request often scrawled on bathroom stalls. (Again, use your imagination.)

Instantly Siri sneered back at him, "Richard, watch your language!"

And that apparently that shut him up.

Not a f you! Not a b me! Not a stick it up you know where. No c-word or any of its derivatives aimed at the uber-prudish Ms. Siri. Nothing. A blank air balloon coming out of my old pal's slack-jawed mouth.

The man was Ivoried. A 99 and 99/100% pure mouth-washing drone of a smackdown.

And in the unearthly silence that followed Siri's commanding admonishment I imagine two things happening that afternoon:

1. Soapy bubbles slowly wafting out of Richard's open mouth, thousands of them soaring up over the breathtaking skyline of Manhattan and into the heavens.

2. After a seven second delay, a guttural sound coming down from those same heavens, rumbling up the L.I.E, echoing through the Midtown Tunnel, drifting down 2nd Avenue, and slowly forming into my sainted Aunt Miriam's disembodied voice raining down on my old pal's upturned face "Shut the front door, ya bleepin' blankety blank!"

VIVIAN MANNING-SCHAFFEL

Vivian Manning-Schaffel is a journalist, essayist and rabblerouser who writes for a vast array of publications like *Jezebel, Working Mother, US Weekly, Time Out New York* and many others. She lives and works in Brooklyn with her husband and two kids.

ON WHAT MAKES A NEW YORKER: ADVICE FOR TAYLOR SWIFT

Vivian Manning-Schaffel

Oh, Taylor. I kind of like you. I really do! I like you even more now that you've announced you're donating a good sum to our public schools. They really need the dough. But please ... stop. Just ... stop.

There's plenty about you that's impressive: You write your own songs. You're as stunning as a supermodel. You don't dress like a hooker. You work hard, seem congenial and have some real talent.

But don't get it twisted: Your appointment to global ambassador of our city doesn't anoint you into authenticity. It just underlines the fact that our beloved New York has eroded into something far more Mall of America than Metropolis; a capital of consumerism where everything's for sale and anything can be bought. Unfortunately, our jaded, tired, black hearts aren't for sale. It's nice that you love our city, but it's hubris of the highest order to think any real New Yorker will buy what you're selling in this capacity. I mean, you've lived here for what — five minutes? I have skin tags that've lived in this city longer than you.

Many moons ago, I came to just New York like you did, albeit a foot shorter and a lot poorer. Young, green, full of vim and vigor, I was blinking into the neon lights, entranced by the cacophony of sights and sounds, full of determination to lift a metaphorical leg and mark my territory. It's even way better for you than it ever was for me: You can afford Opening Ceremony. You can slink into a town car, head out to Roberta's and chonk right into a pile of designer carbs, free of the prying eyes of the paparazzi. You actually own your home and have an epic career, instead of a couch you've surfed on for the three months and the shitty, remedial office job you had to take to pay way too much money for it.

You can throw all the money in the world at us, but calling yourself a "New Yorker" must be earned. I've been here for over seventeed years plus an initial stint in college and am still considered an interloper. A zillion dollar West Village tax write-off with views, a garage, elevator and doorman does not make you a New Yorker. Hanging out in Brooklyn with Lena Dunham does not make you a New Yorker.

When we think of New York, we think of Lou Reed. We think of Joan Rivers. We think of Jocelyn Wildenstein. We think of Robert DeNiro. We think of Al Sharpton. We think of Lady Gaga. We even think of Lena Dunham. In fact, we totally think of Lena Dunham.

Like the mafia, there's no easy way in or out. You have to do a lot of time here to earn your stripes. And you have to actually walk the streets, you can't just take it all in from the back of a chauffered Escalade. So what makes a New Yorker?

• Trudging through snowstorms and hurricanes makes you a New Yorker.

• Fearing Ebola, SARS, MERS, and misuggas while you're actively sneezed on in the subway every day makes you a New Yorker.

• Deeply inhaling the urine-scented stench of a subway platform in August makes you a New Yorker.

• Catching the mouse that mocks you with a trail of shit on your stove makes you a New Yorker.

• Knowing you may die and be reincarnated before the next F train comes makes you a New Yorker.

• Waiting two hours for a doctor's appointment and six in an emergency room makes you a New Yorker.

• Watching someone actually defecate on the street makes you a New Yorker.

• Coping with the Darwinian bullshit that is School Choice makes you a New Yorker.

• Schelpping groceries 15 blocks and up three flights of stairs makes you a New Yorker.

When was the last time you did any of those things? Everyone knows you aren't a true New Yorker until a perfect stranger checks you into place. Hopefully, this has brought you a step closer. You're welcome.

Love and a string of random emoticons,

Viv

SUZANNE McCONNELL

Suzanne McConnell is Fiction Editor for the *Bellevue Literary Review*. Twice nominated for the Pushcart Prize, her stories, essays and poems have appeared in such publications as *Poets & Writers*, the *Huffington Post*, the *Hamilton Stone Review*, the *Saint Ann's Review*, *Bellevue Literary Review*, *Calyx* and many others. She teaches writing and literature at Hunter College and is the Scholar/Facilitator for New Jersey's Literature and Medicine programs at the University of Medicine and Dentistry, and at the Department of Veteran Affairs. Currently, she is writing a book on Kurt Vonnegut's advice on writing. Entitled *Vonnegut's Pearls*, it will be published as an e-book by Rosetta Books and in hard cover by Seven Stories Press. Suzanne, who grew up in San Diego, lives in New York City and Wellfleet, Massachusetts with her husband, the sculptor, Gary Kuehn.

HEAVEN ON EARTH

Suzanne McConnell

They had been about to fall asleep, her head in the crook of his arm. Jed asked "What about it, Maggie, you staying here or are you going back to New York?"

She froze.

Yes, there's this bond between us, yes yes, she yearned to say.

She had struggled to build a self, a life, and it seemed he was asking her to give it up. In her marriage, nine years ago, she had not yet had a life when she had given it up. And that had ended in suicide.

She'd had a series of dreams since meeting Jed. She thought of them as the robber dreams. Someone male broke in to her apartment. Adolescent boys, usually. They'd break down the front door and rush in gleefully. Or burst in through the windows. They'd climb the building and hoist themselves through French doors facing the street. The night after she and Jed quarreled, those doors were wide open.

Jed turned to her. "I'm asking you, Maggie. Stay here with me."

"I would love to, I've fallen in love with you. But … "

She would have to give up dancing with Moving Earth. The company would be returning from Europe in two weeks to resume fall rehearsals. She loved Kai Takei, the director. From the time she took Moving Earth's summer workshop in Vermont, her life began to quicken, as if she had been an animal caved in hibernation and at last had come the end of winter. She'd moved to New York to join the company. It had inspired her to take every kind of bodywork class she could, and work whatever job to afford them and to dance. Moving Earth had given her substance. Maggie wasn't interested in dancing with any other company; she doubted if other companies would be interested in her.

She told him, "I'd have to quit dancing."

"I can't ask you to do that. It'd be like you asking me to give up flying." Jed looked away. "There must be dance companies in San Francisco."

"In November we're scheduled for Vancouver. In December we're dancing at La Mama Theater. "

"There's someone else."

"No."

He waited.

"It's New York. It's not the glamour," she said. "It's the street life. You can't find its equivalent anywhere in the U.S.A. People walk. Life is vivid and all around you, not behind glass and hubcaps. Every size, shape, race, nationality and attitude rubbing up against every other.

"In the spring, my God," she said, "you should see Washington Square and Central Park. Magicians, tightrope walkers, tortoise racers, mimes. All manner of musicians. Everyone moving, skateboarding, jogging, cycling, riding in horse-driven carts. And the streets themselves. Where I live there are still cobblestones, Jed. I wake up to mounted policeman clip-clopping along. I don't know how to tell you what all that means to me."

It had taken her a long time to get used to Manhattan. Coming from the mountains of Vermont to live in no-man's-land downtown, above Wall Street and below Canal, amongst enormous, austere buildings intended for commerce. You had to walk a mile to fetch groceries from the Village or Chinatown, and haul them home by cart.

Now Soho, the adjacent neighborhood, which had been the avant-garde step-sister of the 57th Street art establishment in the early seventies, was flourishing and hot, and that heat was catching on downtown. Artists who'd lived in commercially zoned spaces behind black shades were emerging into the legit light of day through Artist-in-Residence designations. Lawyers were buying lofts. A 24-hour Food Emporium was going up. Fancy restaurants. Even Magoo's, the funky neighborhood hang-out whose owner bartered for art, let you keep a tab, and bought you a drink and a burger when you paid it— had upscaled: new pool table, paint.

"People are beginning to call it TriBeCa, short for Triangle Below Canal. Cab drivers are finding their way. Shoe repair and laundromat won't be far behind. I pioneered that territory, broke the sod, and now I want to reap the rewards."

"This area has a name," Jed said. "The Pastures of Heaven."

"I know. I read your Steinbeck. It is heaven," she said. "But in this heaven you have to get in a car."

EILEEN PALMA

Eileen Palma has a dual B.A. in English and Education from the University of Massachusetts, Amherst and is an alumnus of The Writing Institute at Sarah Lawrence College. Her writing has appeared in *The Momoir Project, Mumaspire, Romance at Random, Blogging in the Big Apple,* and *Macaroni Kid Bronxville.* Eileen is the author of the romantic comedy *Worth the Weight,* published by Diversion Books, and Running Press will soon publish *The Popularity Pact,* a duology about former best friends who make a deal to help one another get in with the "cool" kids, first at summer camp, then at school. Eileen is living out her happily-ever-after in Westchester with her college sweetheart husband Doug, their tween daughter Molly and their scrappy Wire Hair Fox Terrier Oscar.

THE MOSKOWITZ GIRL

Eileen Palma

Eileen Elizabeth, Kathryne Anne, Mary Beth. My sisters and I had first names that depicted our Irish Catholic halves. But the priest couldn't get past our last name. Moskowitz.

"Isn't there anyone else?" he asked our CCD teacher. The ghost of Italy haunted his New York accent.

"Katie and Eileen are the only ones who can actually read the bible passages," the teacher whispered.

"We can't have the Moskowitz girls do the First Communion readings." We still got picked, but only after every other kid butchered the passages. Eastchester was full of Italian-Catholics who had emigrated from Italy by way of the Bronx, with surnames ending in vowels and enviously thick black hair and olive skin. We couldn't afford to live in Scarsdale where Moskowitzes were a dime a dozen. Not to mention, Catholic girls with Jewish last names wouldn't fit in there either.

My father didn't think twice about signing a paper agreeing

to raise his children Catholic so he could give my mom a church wedding. After my grandfather's sisters and mother died in a concentration camp in Hungary, while he was safely ensconced in Mount Vernon, survivor's guilt caused his faith to seep out of him. With no one to guide him, my father forgot all the Hebrew words he had memorized and closed the door on his Jewish life after his Bar Mitzvah.

My mother spent our childhood exploring alternative faiths. We went to meditation classes and bought chunks of crystals that promised to open our chakras and maybe even help with my asthma. Our house came with a cement Virgin Mary statue in the front yard like many of the houses in our neighborhood. After twelve years of Catholic school, my mom was too superstitious to throw out a statue of the Blessed Mother. Our back yard was filled with round-bellied Buddhas and Ganesh, the elephant-headed deity. We lived a life far more suited to New Paltz than Southern Westchester, but that would be too far of a commute for my father who was a New Rochelle fire captain.

The priest always knew who missed church. My mother said he was just keeping track of the collection envelopes.

"If the priest asks why you weren't there, tell him we go to Grandad's church in Tarrytown," my mother told Katie and I when my parents didn't feel like dropping us off.

Katie nodded and ran off to play with her Cabbage Patch Dolls. But, I was certain that lying to a priest would land me in Hell.

A few weeks later, the priest pulled me aside and asked,

"Eileen, why haven't you and your sisters been at church?"

What's worse getting grounded or eternal damnation? I blurted out "Because my mother doesn't want to get up in the morning to take us!" The priest headed down to Katie's classroom next and asked the same question. The answer slid off her tongue, "Father, we go to our Grandad's church every Sunday."

When we swapped stories in our rusted Chevy Blazer that day, I got in trouble for selling my sister out.

My father worked overtime at the firehouse to get us gifts, but he never got into having a Christmas tree. He would drag the artificial tree up from the basement and assemble the color-coded branches while swearing under his breath. Then he would disappear while my sisters and I hung the ornaments with my mom. He did, however, make the best Challah bread French toast on Christmas morning.

When I asked my father why we didn't celebrate Hanukkah and Christmas like my friend who got eight days of gifts and a visit from the North Pole, he told me that Jewish people don't believe in Jesus. "You can't be half-Jewish. It's a religion, not a nationality. You can't celebrate Jesus' birthday one week and be Jewish the next."

At 23, I took my husband's last name, ironically an Italian one, and spent years living everywhere but Westchester, where people only knew me as Eileen Palma. And slowly, my half-Jewish self slipped away. It was only after I moved to Bronxville and opened my Facebook profile as Eileen Moskowitz-Palma that I became whole again.

EDWARD McCANN

Edward McCann is an award winning writer/producer and the founder and editor of *Read650*, celebrating the spoken word with live events in New York City and throughout the tri-state area. A longtime contributing editor to *Country Living*, his features and essays have been published in many literary journals, anthologies, and national magazines, including *Better Homes & Gardens, Good Housekeeping, The Irish Echo, The Sun,* and others. His essay, "Pregnant Again," was selected for the anthology, *Listen To Your Mother*, published by Penguin, and he's recently completed a memoir about the search for his missing nephew. He lives and writes in a pastoral spot about eighty miles north of New York City, and is at work on a collection of essays about life in the Hudson River Valley.

PREGNANT AGAIN

Edward McCann

"When I found out I was pregnant with you," Mom told me, "pregnant again, for the sixth time—I wanted to walk into the ocean until my hat floated."

So. It turns out my conception was not deliberate.

By the time I was conceived in late June 1962, there were already five children at home, ranging in age from a brand new high school graduate to a toddler of fifteen months. I am the third son and my parents' youngest child, the one my mother called her "caboose," the last car on the freight train of my family.

Mom was forty-two and my father nearing fifty when I was born. Now ninety-four, wheelchair-bound, and widowed for as long as she was married, Mom has often told me how much she loves and appreciates me—how "God surely knew what he was doing" when he sent me so late in her life. Still, I can't forget that sense of desperation she once expressed, the hopelessness behind even that momentary suicidal impulse, the image of a pregnant, Irish-Catholic Queens housewife drowning herself like Virginia Woolf, perhaps weighting herself down, as Virginia did, with rocks in her coat pockets, and with me—or, rather, the cluster of cells that might have become me—in her womb.

The idea is especially disturbing because it's so easy to imagine, and Mom wouldn't have had to travel very far before she got her feet wet; Broad Channel, the provincial island town where my family lived, was surrounded by water on all sides—an anomaly—more fishing village than New York City, with Jamaica bay and the nearby Atlantic always present in the salt air, the scream of the gulls, the fog that sometimes rose up around us.

No child wants to imagine his or her conception, but I do, just this once: I count months backward from my birthday. I use the Internet to check historic weather conditions, moon cycles, and tide charts. And then I travel back in time, becoming a fly on the wall on that mild spring night as my soon-to-be parents climbed the stairs of their house on the Boulevard. The children are all in their beds. Dad, feeling frisky, pats Mom's rump as they climb the stairs, a signal she knows well and which I imagine fills her with dread.

George and Mildred are not hoping to produce another child, another mouth to feed. But though Mom is tired and pre-menopausal, Dad has his needs and Mom her wifely duties—duties her mother informed her about shortly before Mildred's wedding some twenty years past. Still a blushing teen, Mildred sat stock still with her hands covering her mouth as she finally learned the long overdue facts of life and the indignities she would have to endure as a married woman.

A light breeze off the bay ruffles the polyester sheers of my parents' screened bedroom windows. By the dim light of the moon, George takes his pleasure behind a locked door beneath the crucifix hanging above the bed. Mildred, meanwhile, closes her eyes and says a silent decade of the rosary, a meditation that transports her away from her body for as long as necessary.

My parents married young, created a home and a family, and they shared their happiness and sorrows. Yet it sometimes seemed to me that Mildred's life—her marriage and her six children—was something that just happened to her, and perhaps wasn't the life she might have chosen if she'd ever believed she had a choice.

"I wanted to walk out into the ocean until my hat floated."

Pregnant again. I try to imagine the different, perhaps sunnier landscape into which Mom's first child was born, the time before my mother's life became an unending laundry cycle, the days unfurling one after the other like an endless potato peel. And then I recall my childhood visits to Far Rockaway beach—the Irish Riviera—where Mom taught me to swim and, eventually, how to relax enough to lie back and ride atop the waves like she did, eyes closed and hands clasped behind her head, her face turned toward the sun.

DAN ZEVIN

Dan Zevin is a Thurber Prize-winning humorist. He has written eight books, including *Dan Gets a Minivan* and *The Day I Turned Uncool*, which were both optioned by Adam Sandler. Dan has been an award-winning humor columnist for the *New York Times*, a comic commentator for *NPR*, and a contributor to print or digital editions of the *New Yorker, McSweeney's, Rolling Stone, Salon*, the *Los Angeles Times, Real Simple*, and *Parents*, among others. He currently teaches comedic writing at Sarah Lawrence College. Dan's latest project is a series of picture-book parodies featuring adorably annoying adults, including *Mr. Selfie, Little Miss Overshare, Mr. Humblebrag*, and *Little Miss Basic*. Dan lives with his wife, kids, and pet rabbit in the suburbs of New York City, where he has become an active member of his local Costco.

SUBURBED:
HOW IT HAPPENED TO US

Dan Zevin

I'm locked out of my locker at the town pool.

I'm wearing a wet bathing suit, goggles, and Sponge Bob flip-flops I stole from the Lost and Found. When the fire engine pulls up, all the kids at the town pool rush over to the fence. They think there's a fire. But the fireman doesn't have a hose. He has a lock cutting apparatus that looks like a giant hedge clippers.

He's a nice fireman. He doesn't look at me funny because he is wearing a firefighting uniform and I am wearing Lost and Found flip-flops. He is a fireman of few words.

"You're from the city," he says. It's not a question, he just knows.

And then:

"You know, you don't have to lock here."

We are living in another family's house. It comes with their driveway, their yard, their furniture, their DVDs, their X-Box and their town pool. We're here courtesy of craigslist, summer rentals, keyword: central air-conditioning.

One summer earlier. Brooklyn. We're not enjoying ourselves. We are not having the Summer of Love. We're having the Summer of Sam, named in honor of our latest neighbor, Sam, who's renting a room in the town house attached to ours. Sam takes his crazy pill every night at 2 a.m. He spends the subsequent hours screaming very bad words at his girlfriend.

One night our kids wake up crying when the domestic violence unit shows up. Don't worry, they tell us. It turns out his "girlfriend" is actually a computer monitor. Until he can be evicted, they have a solution. We should close our windows. We have another potential solution: Suburbia.

Six summers earlier, Megan and I have just moved to Brooklyn. We find our dream home: a cozy, brick town house in a gentrifying neighborhood of Brooklyn. Gentrify-ING, meaning the ratio of bail bond offices to organic, free-range ice cream shops is still about 3:1. But the important thing is, the ice cream is to die for. Our only dependent is a dog, and everyone we meet is incredibly friendly and interesting and a freelance graphic designer.

The one thing left to gentrify in our neighborhood is our neighborhood school. The Department of Education has released something called "School Report Cards." Our neighborhood school does not exactly pass with flying colors. This is what we tell ourselves: We'll cross that bridge when we come to it. After all, this is the city, and we are part of something special. Here, our kids have museums and theater and artisanal, cruelty-free pizza. And single pressed vacuum brewed multi-racial espresso. And what else? Walking! It's good for them to be able to walk everywhere because walking builds up their leg muscles, especially when they break into a wild sprint down Atlantic Avenue like ours do, barely escaping their daily hit and run by the kamikaze driver of bus 63 to Park Slope.

Which probably wouldn't be such a bad thing anyway, because the only way children learn is from firsthand experience, so getting hit by a bus will be an important part of their education—a teaching moment. Yes, getting hit by a bus in Brooklyn will make our kids street smart, not just book smart, we tell ourselves. And that, we tell ourselves, is going to give them a huge advantage over all those sheltered, shallow children from the suburbs.

Megan and I are in the centrally air-conditioned family room of our summer rental in Westchester. We're watching our eight-year-old out the window, transfixed. He's been in that tree for like twelve straight minutes. He climbed it yesterday, too, and the day before that. Sometimes the kid across the street comes over and they climb it together. They just sit in it. They just sit in the tree, they don't even try to push each other off.

This is not how outdoor recreation is conducted back in Brooklyn, I recall. In Brooklyn, there is a compelling argument for population control known as Carroll Park. Carroll Park is the kind of full-occupancy destination that's all fun and games until your children are trampled to death. One day, I remember telling my kids that's it—no more playing in the playground part of Carroll Park. So we check out the rest of the park. We find a quiet garden. It has some trees and a big rock. Leo climbs one of the trees. He's happy up there. He's content. Next thing I know, he's in tears. An old lady with a mustache and an apron that says "Carroll Park Greening Committee" is yelling at him to get down. I tell her to relax and she starts yelling at me.

"Your children are not supposed to be climbing trees!" she says.

Sometimes when Megan and I watch our kids from our family room window today I think about that old hag.

Your children are not supposed to be climbing trees.

If I knew then what I know now, this is what I would have said:

Yes they are.

ACKNOWLEDGMENTS

We thank Nancy Manocherian's the cell, which supported Read650 at its inception. A twenty-first century salon in the heart of New York City, their mission is to support the arts and incubate new works, and the cell made its beautiful performance space available to Read650 as we were finding our way. The cell: To mine the mind, pierce the heart, and awaken the soul.

TheCellTheatre.org

Artists Without Walls was created to inspire, uplift, and unite people and communities of diverse cultures through the pursuit of artistic achievement, and has supported and encouraged Read650 from its beginnings. Artists Without Walls: No Limits. No Walls. No Boundaries.

ArtistsWithoutWalls.com

We're grateful for the support and encouragement from The Writing Institute at Sarah Lawrence College, which supplies a steady stream of excellent writers to Read650. The Writing Institute helps writers in all genres progress and grow in their craft and welcomes them all into a very supportive community.

SarahLawrence.edu

READ650.COM

INFO @READ650.COM
FACEBOOK.COM/READ650

www.ingramcontent.com/pod-product-compliance
Lightning Source LLC
Chambersburg PA
CBHW072045170626
46811CB00008B/3175